MAVOR'S BONES

BY ROLLI

8th House Publishing
Montreal, Canada

Published in Canada by 8th House Publishing.
Front Cover Artwork by Rolli (Charles Anderson)

Designed by 8th House Publishing.
www.8thHousePublishing.com

Set in Adobe Garamond Pro, Always Here and Perpetua.

Library and Archives Canada Cataloguing in Publication

Rolli, 1980-, author
        Mavor's bones : a Gothic novel-in-poems / Rolli (Charles Anderson).

ISBN 978-1-926716-30-5 (pbk.)

        I. Title.

PS8635.O4465M39 2014   C811'.6   C2014-904408-9

MAVOR'S BONES
A Gothic Novel-in-Poems

by
ROLLI

for my family

may they rest   in peace

CONTENTS

Dear Mother

My Mother

II. Company's Come

Mother Bird

IV. Confessional

V. Hymns of a Sexton

So I Lie. My
Eulogy
Style's That That
I Can Almost See Home
Bones
We Leaves
Dead King's Bridge
Blue Angel
Hymns of a Sexton
The Old Philosopher II
Twilit Minuet
The Sadness Has Passed Hasn't
I Am Become One Rose
I Am No Poet, Only
Heart Song

Notes
Bio

Mavor's Bones

Rolli

DEAR MOTHER

above

if you could see
me dear mother
*   in your bitterness*

*   my clothes*

if you could see
*   my poverty*

if we could meet
dear mother

*   and soon*

and you'd time
my mother
in bitterness
to listen

in sickness, and
set

down your cigarette

listen

we'd fix
which didn't
respire
in lifetime, my
mother
of smoke

oh my mother, might
lie
in soft ashes
and warm, softly
talking
    and talking

Dear mother
    blind
to my poverty
be

as one moth-
er
unborn

together

    and wealthy again

I. SEPTEMBER'S WHEN

The Orangery Tree

4

grew
through roof of glass
to Mavor's room
who pruned it
once
    and tenants bed, bent-
boned

The breeze steals
in

the cold

an orange, spor-
adically

leaves
that green the sun

They tend
me
mending
less
    and less

Rolli

5

My cross
grown orange
glints in
companioning

And yet

there's something wonderful

to lean outside, in spring

the overfoaming white

and the sound of the sea

She Has Become the Ocean

I have   been dreaming

I have been   remembering

I have been dreaming
those dreams   of meaning
that come from the waters
of dreaming   deep
like drowned men
to the gold skin
of the ocean

I have been remembering

For there is more   of water
in thought   and bend
than an arm   of the ocean
more   in thought   of one
than the whole   of ocean

Rolli

She has become the ocean
that edges every
thing
her phantom as the water
of viridian

She has become
the ocean
the folding over
main
the universal water
* of viridian*

The Old Philosopher I

So the bones
rose up
summing one
academician

    cigarette in hand

A pleasure, now and then, to stand

Ah, to see
of a gloom-
y route home
the bohemian

    sauntering out the tomb

There was too little elbow-room

Recluse (The Duke)

Recluse
they've named me

chilled   to wine
              society

If
I cupboard me
what man grasps hand-
les
passes drink?

Think

those collisions of friends
each spending   a word
afterwards grunting
of the other's thrift

And it seems
to scold for distance is
to throw a child
     and motive his screams

         Though I am
         but one
         obtuse

     recluse

Rolli

September's When

the poets grow
old
alter colour
    and fall

thou mayest in me

    Years
have I dyed my
grey

Please—re-
serve your sympathy for thieves
of beauty, whose
stealings stole backs
    and plug stomachs

        the green-
        grocers, folders
        of wheat
        the clean cutters
        of sheep

A minute
fills
with shovels
whales
of these
    brittling thieves

Keep harvesting

Boy with a Ball

From the shadow, yellow wall
                    of a tree steals
boy and ball

He was there a week, and
                centuries ago
says Grandam (who should know)
it was plague that thinned him
till he fit
that bit of churchyard earth
that fits us all
It must have been—
he lingers in the fall

Hmm? The meadow, somewhere
            in the meadow's heart
                    The greenest part

My De-

ceased poems
which lived in me
as dreaming
meet

They patient
in
for mo-
ment which
    elapsed them

        As light
        in hand
        as light

and can

you feel them?

Grief is Meat

Grief   is meat   is gravy
for the brain   to stew in

Less   its fattening   we'd   be
as much calcium   as them
who we abandoned   by living

Grief   is meat   of Lent
the empty   man

the vegetarian

the pig   on a spit

     Too rich for pity   it

The Old Matriarch

"She died   so many years
ago
(at least an even score)
and left us an Egyptian
rug
we lay outside the door
to dry the feet of credit-
ors,
we'd say, and laugh away"

"I'm glad she's dead" said May

"The Duke   was at her bedside
when the angels   claimed
her soul
and through the open shutters
touched
the jasmine
on the wall
collecting blooms enough the toll
to pay   at God's gateway"

"A load o' *bull*" said May

"A Venus (in her younger
years)
de Milo (but with arms)
and not one suitor   in a group
could neutralize her charms.
They'll come to *you*
in swarms
one day
Renée"

"WHERE'S MY WHEELCHAIR?" raged May

tossing sugar tongs

THE STRANGE GODDESS

In those days Grassini sang at the Opera, and her voice
was delightful to me beyond all that I had ever heard.
                                        —de Quincey

I lived
as addict
and
his medicine

Inspiration
is a strange goddess

fire balloon
eluding one
for months

or courting
touch, but

changing

    rain

      on awed
      skin

I sought her
everywhere

    and everywhere
    the same

Rolli

I wrote, only
scrapes
on paper
songless
orange
    in my throat

So I paused
in cold rooms
warmed
by breath
of men

    spinning wind in-
    to paper

The better
for my health
by far

I've since then lived
a still
life

    grown grey

    and lazy

I seldom remember her

My Lady in Heaven

My lady in heaven
hallowed be
and lighter than
when your circle was the sun

A chill   or when
a quick depression
sinks the room
     a sexton going
     smoke
or a pill-bottle falls
unaccountably, lady

I fold my hands
remembering

     But only then

The clock runs
down
the sun
and white-robed chemists running
home
rub eyes

     and sigh for my lady in heaven

My Old Age Came

as shaves of dusk

    a soot-fall piling

I have
been Ramses
in glass
    but subtly living
    impotent

the head
on the wall
privy to one
room's gossip
    the revolutions
    of a glass eye

My death
will break like rain

    or a single ray

Rolli

Autumning

Again
the melanchol-
y autumning

my brain
in cupboard of
spring

Beneath these
leaves
me be-
lieve

    but
      un-
    brained
      and wait-
    ing

        wait

May wake
me please
in May

and shake

these

leaves

Mavor's Bones

I Have a Yellow Bird

that drinks
from my finger

feather

the wind-
ow wind
blew in

Its nourishing
me feeds
    its singing

prick

the skin

and thin

    my passion

Rolli

To Live In Green Glass

one must tempt friends
into ovens, shutting
doors, remorseless

must line one's sons
and scythe them
like the autumn
wheat

must slough clothes
become brutal, duel
in clay for day's
entertainment

One must then
ascend
a tall bottle, fall
deep
the chimney-sweep
in

this inhabit till
dry, the glass
and smash with clenched
fists

If one lives, it's
to hit
on a bottle, start
again

the echo till
death / checked
by watchers

mocking god

god pleading re-
lease
from green glass

Rolli

My Mother

above me
hear

    for my clothes
    are so broken
    my mother

      if there is
      a mother
      above

oh listen
my mother

for one dust
in millions brushing
one

Mother

can it be

the sweat
of life
    the trophy

oh mother
be

    deficiency

this lightness
in
the light of dusk
my mother

be

    this frailty?

Say
it may not
be

    this justice

Whisper
say
it may not be

    but rushing dream
    my mother

    but amazing dream

II. Company's Come

C OMPANY ' S C OME

and the worms urge together
     I'll with fishhooks prick them, lift
see white teeth see

I'll pinch, with pincer-fingers
the decanter
     and slant it till spilled

When I lax my jaw, gas
will fall out polished
and vocabulary

          pass epigrams
          gnawing off ends

          touch hair
          the vacancy there

          breathe war
          gust guests out the door

bye-bye

and silent, nearly, sitting
     a shrill picked by insects
teeming in their million sea

Rolli

UNCLE REGINALD (REGGIE)

the vegetarian
postcard-thin
a sailor in his neon years
forever saying clever
things

To tell a man's honest?
Simple—skim his eyes
They should be quite swollen

Colourful life, mine
black lamb with blue
devils telling
white
lies

He played with children
nine and ten
    and passed his last
years in the pen

Old News

And how's it going
Old News?

We've not forgotten you

We've not forgotten
    really
it's a whistling season

Oh—Old News

who's done

        —what others do newly
        and with more hair

        —such wonders
        as happen—annually, perhaps

It's been *awfully* long

What? We *need*? Mirrors?
With fewer wrinkles?

Droll, O.N., droll

Still

there's a few who'd
scratch scalp

We won't, Old News

If you ever need

Mmm hmm

If you *ever*

Mmm hmm
Mmm hmm

If you ever need *anything*

Mmm hmm
Mmm hmm
Mmm hmm
Mmm hmm
Mmm hmm

Toodle-oo

I Should, To Die, Like the By

to be eating peach

on chin-drip slipping

off the yacht

The Philosopher Talks

Though he'd spent the better part of his life rummaging through libraries, the philosopher assured us he'd learned only two things in that time: that the human race is, and has always been, essentially happy; and that it's impossible to convince anyone of the fact.

"We are now happier," he said, refilling his glass, "than any period in history. Observe our luxuries, and conveniences. Our *medicine,*" laughing. "Observe if you will the poor, who live, compared to those of a generation or two ago, like—if not pharaohs, at least tomb-robbers. And so each generation has some advantage over last, can look over its shoulder and say, 'Well, we have Plague, but not floods,' 'rats, but not Plague,' '*small* rats, not large ones,' or, in our own time, 'ten varieties of hothouse oranges to pick from, rather than a measly seven.' And all the while, rats or no, there is flesh and novels and walking to pubs and being carted home and all things that make life liveable.

"And yet," buttering the biscuit, "slinking into all this good cheer is—a melancholy *shadow*. It will try always, and always fail, in its own time, to catch our notice, to dim an instant of our happiness. Resentful, it slips back into its crack in the wall. It dreams its melancholy dreams. It spins them into paper, like a widow spider.

"A century may pass, or two. In fact, it *will*. And some tomb-robber or other, digging, will discover them—the dreams and scribblings of a long-gone shadow. And he will say, this digger, 'Ah! The spirit of the age was *bitterness*. It was … despair," when this is not so. Yet when men adore—and they will—these discovered dreams, these novelties, they are poisoning themselves, only. When they write of them, or speak, they are poisoning *others*. The dreams of the shadow become our own dreams. We *are* happy, though we live in a dream. It is the ultimate glory of the shadow.

"Consider Valé's *Charnel Poems*, written during one of his many stays in the asylum. Can there be any doubt that it will, one day, be said to characterize the present age? Because, you know," chuckling, "we all go around digging up corpses and eating them. May I have another biscuit?"

Rolli

I Now Am a Skeleton

I now am   a skeleton

Your hands   I will shake   and
thank
you my critics
for picking   me   clean

     For meat   is as grass

     and needs cutting

I light am   and smooth   as true
bone
china

My teacup
seats   upon me   speaks
of my new utility

     For my work

     was but purpose   of life

     and the broth   of my vein

I must give you again
my critics my digital
hand

It is crucial   use
of human time
your cutting   cunning
truly

    For I do   not mind my
    vision
    or my hearing being
    taken   with my taste
    when I have gained
    my critics   dis-
    tinction:

    being the being
    more
    in your morning
    mirrors

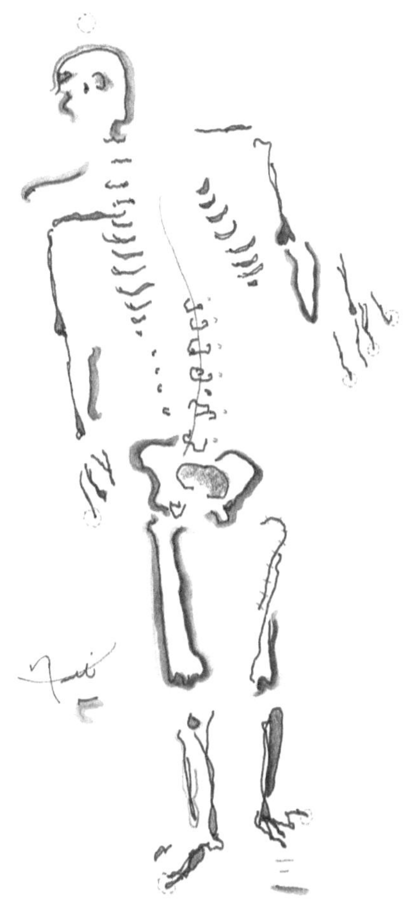

Such Vineyards

If muted
you
what humours
you
of me
believe
we
will in
such vineyards
live
of stillness
we
will even
see
within
the mu-
ted vines

the embryo of wine

Rolli

Reputation (Uncle Reggie Said)

is a twin of one, but
less moral
more sociable
crass
a tosspot charlatan (on
the whole—an ass)

Third Persons

When sadness *had* us
when it   finished with us
and there was nothing   but *something* of
us
    our widow skin

when it   unclasped us   sadness
collapse   as a wasp's fall
was silent   as nightfall

when it   quit us   hiss
of a tongued machine   the steaming
word   birds   became
of grey   escaping

when it *left* us   we remained

When grief leaves   we remain

Bereaved   of leaves
the tree remains   a tree

It feels
more easily   its skin
the teething   wind
    its mothering

When grief leaves we   remain
and altering we

are not   reborn
or curtained
but   third persons

learning   speech   again
to work   the limbs
to sing

Felicity   is pain
We'll sing again

Throats   are thickening
We'll sing again

Words are jars of rain

        We'll sing again

43

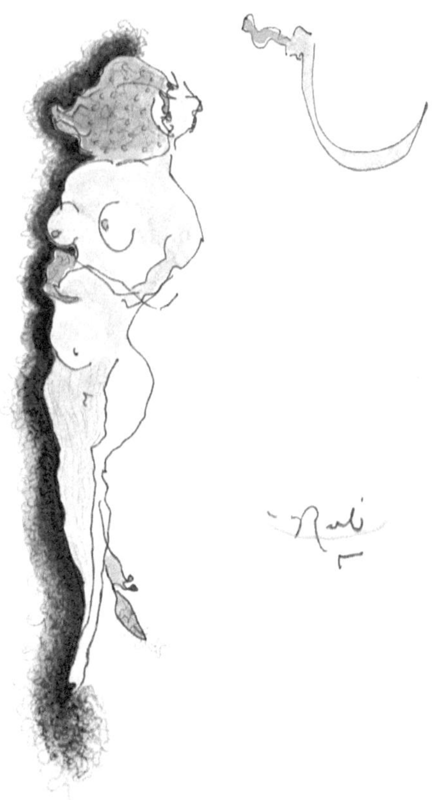

Chauffeur

Chauffeur earl-
y me
to cemetery

the hole
my gold pour
in

and burn
the skeleton

Orangutan

Grandam
in afghan
said again

I was reaching—he
in green-leaved shadow more brown
than orange—for oranges

His lips stripped back
     to black

An ocean   in the ear

          I woke in here

Uncle John

Any odd day, John's
in the wine cellar smelling
    a bottle bottom
    history book
an orange from the orangery floor
(perhaps a whore)

His wife once said, *What's
his aim, late nights
when he steps out the door?*

She wonders no more
    and lives in Champagne Tenement
    the first floor, number four

Of Age

But doub-
ly fun
to grey
disgrace-
fully

PASTIMES

A chair and Aunt May
whose view through the
bay
was the west side door
as day as perfume of a whore wore
away

There

From the shadow, hat
and whisker (with
a man attached)
moved rat-like to the door
    and scratched

There

He eyed eye-
shadow
negligée
flambé
(Renée)

*He'll stay   till ten
    then
as many tens lighter
go
    I know*

Rolli

She'll clean   an hour
at least   but these
anatomies
impure the washing bowl

The parlour sees the
artistry
the keyhole   the soul

I Know It is Only

the breathing
sea
that wakes me

only
the sea
that wakes me
    though

I throw
my sheet
    and breathing
in

    I listen

Mother Bird

It's middle of night
again   again
bless us moth-
er
in littleness
with

sing us
through
the waiting

till day

Can you hear
and not see
us mother   bird-
less the season
hear

us mother

feel

us

smoothing

soothe

through the night?

III. Boneyard Stroll

The Duke's Gout
a clipping from *The Whisper*

The Duke's gout rebukes
him
Venison and butter!
so he sits, foot cushioned
and pyjamad in glower

He's passed half his life
so
in ginantonic nap
cracks books but to shut them *What
a satisfying snap!*

There's little that thrills
him
(not his wife's touch
    though I've heard the new serving girl
pleases him much)

He's kind to his mast-
iff
fair to his mother
He's not an old reprobate
    just his big brother

BONEYARD STROLL

Angel, alone. Enter the Philosopher.

"Glum spot for a walk."
"It's quiet."
"So it is. I come here myself, for the same thing.
To think."
"What do you think about?"
"You."

"That's to say, not you *personally*. But the dead
in general."
"I'm not sure what you mean."
"I suppose you know what happens, child, when
people die?"
"They lie in a box. Then they go to heaven."
"And if we dug up the box of ... Abraham, over
here, and opened it, it would be empty—because,
after all, he's gone to heaven?"

"There might be bones."
"Oh?"
"If he didn't go. Not everybody does."
"Do you think *you* will?"
"Yes."
"Did your mother?"
"Oh, yes. Everyone says so."
"Perhaps you'd like to check."

"She's in the vault, child. It would be simple to check."

"I don't want to."

"Ha! Joking. Apologies. Let's talk of something else. I'll bet you know whose grave *this* is."

"He wrote plays, a long time ago. People still go to them. Grandam took me to one, once; there was a ghost in it."

"And *this* one."

"I can't tell. It's … crumbled."

"And I'd wager that, even if the words were still clear, there'd be no one left who could even tell you *who* he was. He might've been a doctor, a banker, a clergyman. Not a poor man, or woman, certainly (it's a rich enough stone; the poor are lucky to get one at all). A wealthy merchant, perhaps. His princely terror of a son. Some gloating local hero, forgotten with the last shovelful of earth. But ah, our playwright. Dig up *his* grave, and I guarantee you'll find nothing, not a single rib. The others, well—it's like they never lived at all. They might as well have been drowned at birth, like kittens."

"Don't look so glum, child! It isn't that terrible a place. In fact, I often come here for amusement; one finds such comical names, sometimes, on the older stones. Cornelia Tongue, there. Edward Crump. Look at this one! Riggle de Vurms. *Riggle de Vurms!* Terrific! Ha ha ha!"

Exit Angel, the Philosopher falling in stitches.

In Cigarette

There notion
is
in cigarette
if only, though
blown
free

There is a Tunnel Somewhere Where

There is a tunnel somewhere where
sleep   the green   ideas
of the geniuses
who missed   an hour   to turn
to words
their verdure

    I'm tunnelling

    for golden vein   of green

    I'm tunnelling

Say Nada

55

of the shovelling
poet

this grunty pigging he thinks
poetry

digging and digging

which opinion's
stanchioned
by pigs:

the rhodian pine my
gardener trimmed
till—where's it?

Say nada when
fin
I bury him, listen-
ing

till bristles still

Crushing, He Said, My Sweat of Life

in the dry earth
for ones unloved by
me

So my jolt of life
in the end
to be pensioned
my toil
with vitriol
in a wide-rimmed
pail
which I carry warily
    not to spill a drop

Not a
not a
nada

To some
it's little
    nothing   but
    little's drudging
with much to be done
    for something
        isn't it?

The price
of vitriol climbs
I'm told

If it holds
the trend
well

     it will be satisfactory

A Glass in the Gallery

Nights
the Duke moved the halls
where lurked precursors

Turning
a rose-eyed portrait in green
the original Duke

whose madness had millennia
of luggage

Sliding the archetype
picking the lock
he filled from the hidden
cupboard the cup

replacing frame
as the sun came up

A Life of Great Gaiety

I have lived
a life of great
gaiety

To praise
have I listened
chin in hand

Flatter me

I challenge
you
        and vanish

The Man

She thought oft-
en of him
  the picture firm

  his face
a changing mist
of skins

finger-
thin, his
limbs

the scarecrow coast-
ting

Mary was
nine
the garden dark-
ening

  *Death
  is one man's
  whim*

She thought often of him

The Dead, Gentlemen

are helpless
without breath

I'll supply it

Recall—your father's father's
knee. *Requiescat IP*. E-
ternity's a year—a hundred, or three—re-
ligion
an instant's concentration

Are they not wonderful, ones
and exact
who crack afterlife
stir up dust, pluck
alabaster, wrappings
cluck *lucky! undisturbed!*
unplundered! (un-
til now) *how he LEERS—or seems—mere*
rigor mortis—oh!

How long
till they stomp con-
secration—cig end
the men—then fin-
gers in earth
haul up your bitter mother
by the collar
jostle her
calling
and the jaw drops off?

Rolli

Plunder becomes—
and necrophily—science
        Convicts pause
as mold grows
wine
to ply them—hero/heroines

None touch them; ones
who might lie
dried, and pinned
grinning
next your unfamiliar skin

in the British Museum

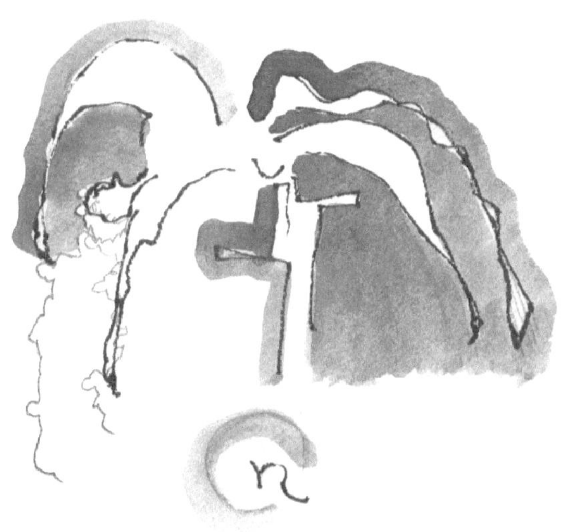

Bequeath Me a Library

and will I
think
of man
the pith

sufficient

There Is So Much of Emotion

There is so much of emotion

    my poet's emotion

It is so marrow
grown
as the swollen brain

If feeling   is green
my feeling   is green
and contained
as the rain-
ing terrarium

If feeling   is rich
my feeling   is rich
as tongues
of the orotund
ocean

As chasm   as ocean

so much

of emotion

My Time in the Desert

was uneventful

Dunes
huger than ingenuity

No mysteries these

Counterfeit visions
        ocean, stone
crumbed to touch

Men
have been thrown so
before

In my tired lust
dust took wings, in
my sun-struck
eyes

A common phenomenon

I stepped from end
to desert end

No one touched me

Not even the devil

65

Wind is My Breathing

Wind   is my breathing

When I close   my thinking

lay over   my brain   with clay

and listen

    there is no division

Wind   has kilned
itself   a self
and plays
at rhapsodies

I So Melancholy Became Again

I   so melancholy became   again
as rain
despite   my promising

There's little in   dry promising
when fogs within   one sit

        and heaven's wet

Don't Think

of me mother of
poverty
sickness

glimpse
from verso of glass at
your room

as it was

the brushes
    clean
the bed
spread pressed
clean as sand

Can you see
me my mother
asleep

but of silent
mind, my
mother
my thin-
king

serene

of field

and green

    sea-green

mid-liquor of dream?

IV. Confessional

Mavor's Bones

Alas, Man

for we
will chipped to
be
at last
our axioms

The Moss Woman

I entering
our garden
of green
moss
saw

the woman

On broad
stone
reposing

Rolli

She
rose

And falling
from
her arms
the dark moss

And beautiful
she moved
on
the grass

And soft-
ly she breathed
in

her tongue
of green
appearing

She
sang
to *me*

I am
so melancholy

Her song
was
such
as men
can *not*
recall

I can
not
recall
her song

It falls
as
moss
from her arm

The wind
lifts

    It is gone

Mary

There

Licked
wet

stretched

in sand

where sand
amends

with wet

We knew
the smooth-
rimed eyes

soft marble

of Mary

Family Poet

There was a poet in the family
    oh yes, a century back, black-
haired, polished com-
post of Polish charm

In groups, he su-
perimposed on guests
sucked colour of wine to dye
his breath—so droll, though
we laughed, only, gassed
as he passed
out the door
    a last time

We found him
flat
on sand
    wrapped
by sun
    posing
bones
of a glass-trapped thing

on thinned lips a lick of
      achievement, serene

We heaped him in sand
      and walked home

Confessional

A brother
Mavor, an
    exception

head
of stretched
wax
candle
bones
    and melting eyes

I could not adapt
to a face
    ate
when he swayed
in braces
ache
    lay abed days
in pain

Don't mention him again

Rolli

Walk With the Philosopher

Ambition (laughed
the Philosopher
burning
the skin
of an orange)
is akin
to murder

For there is
in the end
and our memory
room
for so few

To surpass
a man
is to burn
him
lift
from the earth
him
burn
again him
flick
in wind
from the end
of a cigar-
ette
ash

of his im-
mortality
(laughing
casting
the last
bit of skin)

Amen

She Lived Amid Roses, So

I sought her
suitor
in gardens

One evening meeting
wind
in petals
wet
on thorns

her own
rose
odour
only

Nescience

is end

of many

       and   my solace

I walk often
in gardens

She lives   amid roses

The Tragic Mask

has worn so
long the face
we no more know
the grief
from artistry

Grandam's Dream

I lived
in a star
with our washer-
girl

a Virgo
Star
and gentle-
men
were kissing
me

She? she
screamed
*The leather map
of the Apennines?*

We scratched an hour

There were four starshowers

Yes, the gin

(Or did it happen?)

O PINION

I have kicked   opinion

I will not stick   it again

in my vein

For my breath   is no better
than anyone's smelling
breath

My piss   is the same

And I will listen
to piss   its ring
on porcelain
no more

I am opening the door

    Above   the hum
    of blood
    the beating ear-
    drum

    there is no opinion

Rolli

A Syllable

83

Your wrongs call ac-
complishment
and none   will
chronicle
a syllable

The Garden

A shadow in glass

I can feel it

Watching
the mossed-over grounds
downed columns
the fountain dead of thirst
the girl named Angel stirred
her lips

Tonight

I've often said it, yet

   tonight

Gently closing
the door
skimming fingers
inserting in-
to silent green

When she vanished

The path ran to fog

the garden

A few fronds
juiceless, crisp, sizzled
pots and dropped leaves
the oddments

withered instantly

And the garden's air
   damp grandeur
the monarch on
her deathbed

Rolli

*And wouldn't it be
odd
if it really was*

*after so much watchful standing
back*

walking on

if

At path's end
the fog relented   and

there he was

Yes

Tall

and black

Yes

He held out his hand

Yes

And they walked into fog

If Lived Today Shakespeare, He'd

too milky sea be
dubbed, ob-
scure
to swim

Poor William
I knew him

Brother John (Yellow Letter)

I was born so, shadow-
less, living
the motley of cloth thought
man
by men

yet not myself

Dawn——olive
drab   I shambled
on tile

in glass, on crown
            the edge

Rolli

At the abbey
they greeted me
with stained hands

Now the days
are grape-taking
labour
and song
raising wants
and voices in song

When they sing of god
I sing with them
        unfirm
but listening, singing

Heaven brush us, dust

I think little
of my old life

For consolation, call
it dream
        and half believe it

Brothers—but
they'd shrink
from one among them, un-
deceived

Buttoned, God, we're one

Perhaps
they dwell themselves
restless, tilt-
ing sand

ink paths of sleep
at last
like me

and dream

Perhaps There Will Not Be

in the end   any   singing   and

it   will be

as deep   cathedrals   in

the deep   of evening

Only Bones

lay of anything

Why is it
mother

of bones

the singing
thins

all things

the wonder
mother

grains

remain

remains?

V. Hymns of a Sexton

So I Lie. My

time
on crutch ups
the stair

its drum

welcome
welcome

Eulogy

What
can one say
of May?

She'd squeeze my nose, so firmly, with both
hands, if I disturbed her.

Anything else?

Her purse. She'd stick pins in it, inside out,
till it was … a glistening porcupine. And if
any lax young man were to grab at it—well.
The screams could be heard for weeks.

Something gladder, perhaps?

She mowed over a boy in her chair, once. That's ... the pleasantest thing, I think. Oh—there was the time, near the end, when I found a mint in her Bible—a bill between pages, for pages. When I told her, she said, "Take it. What need could a yellow onion like ME have for money?" So you see, she knew of her harshness. I'm not sure if that makes her a better person, or a worse. The money? Debts, mostly. And jewellery.

What
can *I* say
of May?

Style's That That

stays
when skeleton's
left
for the day

I Can Almost See Home

over hor-
izon

I cry-
ing I

almost
home
see

Please
where was once
be

the memory

agree

Bones

and low the sun

One gummed
and wrung, one
glanced
back
    and the Duke through amber
glass

Ashes (the Vicar)

pages flew

Dust

words turned leaves

See (Gran collap-
sing)

    Something

        leaves

            and nothing

We Leaves

will be the green
of everything

our arteries
a bird

the plums
our afterword

Dead King's Bridge

The Duke
dusty and red, rose
out of the bottle
    and into the night

over knoll
and thorn
the walkway
stone, in-
toning

For the yesterwine of childhood
and the moonlight of my youth
to swallow both as cordially
as——

On Dead King's Bridge
he paused

as boy with new-cut tooth

and poured himself in-
to the river

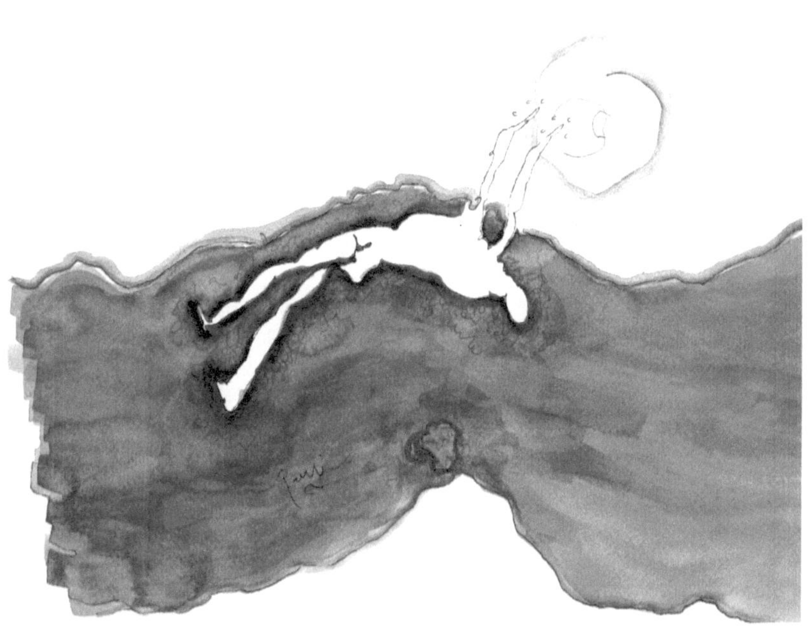

BLUE ANGEL

The blue Angel lay
on sand   an
eye above cloth
    like honest just-
ice

*In heaven I have
no name*

*The stain-
less
godless
and lost
    huddle
        in the middle*

*Our former pur-
pose rushed
away*

*In heaven
    I have no name*

    Thumbs
of tide
on eye-
lids
brushed them
    shut

Hymns of a Sexton

I.

I cover them

Who no one had
will have
one

Who nothing
will be grieved
by one

Who un-
rewarded
one
word
earn

before the turning of the earth

II.

In the cadmiums of earth
and golds
I fold them in
their colouring
I lay them   as the painter lays
his loving   colour
covering

in the amethysts of earth
and greens

the cadmiums

III.

And the earth is warm

In even rain   it is warm
as skin
and mothering:
who cuts us   from   her flesh
in end will bend   to flesh
    again

IV.

The moths are   drawn
      my lantern

I have breathed them in
      as oxygen

I have breathed them in
      and out   again

as man
who earth
will learn
his hymn

and sing again

The Old Philosopher II

So the bones
collapsed
of our laugh-
ing casuist

      grim and ossein

It's so good to be dead again

Rolli

Twilit Minuet

So orange
though
that muted
you
must seem
and me
but so-
lo strut-
ting in
the orangery!

The Sadness Has Passed Hasn't

it

inched
the tur-
ban worm

to some unco-
vered vertex for
a term

I Am Become One Rose

I am become one rose
of the starlit garden

Winter
will we crisp
together

and
the summer rain
soft again

I Am No Poet, Only

burner   of words
I turn
till they pain   my nail

I fill
with ash the ash
pail

Rolli

Heart Song

So it tapped me
companion
*   at last*

Through glass
the branch
and skin inch-
ing

*   A week*
*   a day*
*   an hour, perhaps*
*   may pass*

*   A week*
*   a day*
*   an hour before*
*   at last*

*   a rush of blood*

*   and a sound of wind in glass*

NOTES

DEAR MOTHER
First printing: *Transition* (May 2011).

THE ORANGERY TREE
First printing: *Grain*, VOL. 34, No. 4 (July 2007), as
"Orangery."

SHE HAS BECOME THE OCEAN
First printing: *Transition* (December 2012).

RECLUSE (THE DUKE)
First printing: *Paragon*, VOL. 2 (April 2009), as
"Recluse."

SEPTEMBER'S WHEN
First printing: *Barnwood* (April 2011).

BOY WITH A BALL
First printing: *Grain*, VOL. 34, No. 4 (July 2007).

MY DE-
First printing: *Transition* (June 2014).

GRIEF IS MEAT
First printing: *Transition* (December 2012).

THE STRANGE GODDESS
First printing: *Writing Tomorrow* (October 2013).

MY LADY IN HEAVEN
First printing: *Transition* (December 2012).

I HAVE A YELLOW BIRD
First printing: *Barnwood* (April 2011).

TO LIVE IN GREEN GLASS
First printing: *Barnwood* (2009), as "Green
Bottles."

UNCLE REGINALD (REGGIE)
First printing: *The Egregious*, VOL. 2, No. 2
(February 2009), as "Uncle Reginald."

THIRD PERSONS
First printing: *Transition* (December 2012).

UNCLE JOHN
First printing: *Grain*, VOL. 34, No. 4 (July 2007).

THE DUKE'S GOUT
First printing: *Spring*, VOL. 5 (October 2007), as
"The Duke."

THERE IS SO MUCH OF EMOTION
First printing: *Transition* (December 2012).

DON'T THINK
First printing: *Transition* (May 2011).

FAMILY POET
First printing: *Strange Horizons* (June 2008).

BROTHER JOHN (YELLOW LETTER)
First printing: *subTerrain*, No. 53 (2009), as
"Brother John."

PERHAPS THERE WILL NOT BE
First printing: *Transition* (December 2012).

ONLY BONES
First printing: *Transition* (May 2011).

EULOGY
First printing: *Writer's Eye* (July 2009).
Reprinted: *Feathertale Review* (May 2013).

I CAN ALMOST SEE HOME
First printing: *Transition* (June 2014).

WE LEAVES
First Printing: *CV2*, VOL. 35, No. 4 (April 2013).

DEAD KING'S BRIDGE
First printing: *Spring*, VOL. 5 (October 2007).
Reprinted: *Inscribed*, VOL. 3, No. 1 (February 2008).

HYMNS OF A SEXTON
First printing: *Barnwood* (2013).

HEART SONG
First printing: *Spring*, VOL. 5 (October 2007), as "Mavor's Heartsong."

author photo by Tea Gerbeza

BIO

Rolli is a writer, illustrator and cartoonist hailing from Saskatchewan. He's the author of three short story collections—*I Am Currently Working On a Novel, God's Autobio* and *Dr. Franklin's Staticy Cat*—and *Plum Stuff*, a book of poems. His cartoons appear regularly in *Reader's Digest, Harvard Business Review, Adbusters, The Chronicle of Higher Education* and other popular outlets. Visit Rolli's website—rollistuff.com—and follow him on Twitter @rolliwrites.